SandCastle 2

What Do You See?

On the Prairie

Mary Elizabeth Salzmann

Published by SandCastle™, an imprint of ABDO Publishing Company, 4940 Viking Drive, Edina, Minnesota 55435.

Printed in the United States.

Cover and interior photo credits: Corel, PhotoDisc.

Library of Congress Cataloging-in-Publication Data

Salzmann, Mary Elizabeth, 1968-
       On the prairie / Mary Elizabeth Salzmann.
           p. cm -- (What do you see?)
       ISBN 1-57765-568-0
           1. Prairies--Juvenile literature. [1. Prairies.] I. Title.
    QH87.7 .S26 2001
    578.74'4--dc21   2001022013

The SandCastle concept, content, and reading method have been reviewed and approved by a national advisory board including literacy specialists, librarians, elementary school teachers, early childhood education professionals, and parents.

Let Us Know

After reading the book, SandCastle would like you to tell us your stories about reading. What is your favorite page? Was there something hard that you needed help with? Share the ups and downs of learning to read. We want to hear from you! To get posted on the Abdo Publishing Company Web site, send us email at:

sandcastle@abdopub.com

About SandCastle™
Nonfiction books for the beginning reader

- Basic concepts of phonics are incorporated with integrated language methods of reading instruction. Most words are short, and phrases, letter sounds, and word sounds are repeated.

- Readability is determined by the number of words in each sentence, the number of characters in each word, and word lists based on curriculum frameworks.

- Full-color photography reinforces word meanings and concepts.

- "Words I Can Read" list at the end of each book teaches basic elements of grammar, helps the reader recognize the words in the text, and builds vocabulary.

- Reading levels are indicated by the number of flags on the castle.

Look for more SandCastle books in these three reading levels:

Level 1 (one flag)	Level 2 (two flags)	Level 3 (three flags)
Grades Pre-K to K 5 or fewer words per page	**Grades K to 1** 5 to 10 words per page	**Grades 1 to 2** 10 to 15 words per page

This is a prairie.

Tall grass grows on the prairie.

Some prairies are next
to forests.

Other prairies are near mountains.

This prairie has a stream
running through it.

Many grasshoppers live on the prairie.

Badgers live on the prairie.

They sleep in deep holes.

Antelope live on the prairie.

They run very fast.

Bison live on the prairie.

Bison have thick fur.

What do you see on this prairie?

(rabbit)

Words I Can Read

Nouns

A noun is a person, place, or thing

fur (FUR) p. 19
grass (GRASS) p. 5
prairie (PRAIR-ee)
  pp. 5, 11, 13, 15, 17, 19, 21

rabbit (RAB-it) p. 21
stream (STREEM) p. 11

Plural Nouns

A plural noun is more than one
person, place, or thing

antelope (AN-tuh-lope) p. 17
badgers (BAJ-urz) p. 15
bison (BYE-suhn) p. 19
forests (FOR-istss) p. 7
grasshoppers
  (GRASS-hop-urz) p. 13

holes (HOHLZ) p. 15
mountains
  (MOUN-tuhnz) p. 9
prairies (PRAIR-eez) pp. 7, 9

Verbs

A **verb** is an action or being word

are (AR) pp. 7, 9
do (DOO) p. 21
grows (GROHZ) p. 5
has (HAZ) p. 11
have (HAV) p. 19
is (IZ) p. 5

live (LIV) pp. 13, 15, 17, 19
run (RUHN) p. 17
running (RUHN-ing) p. 11
see (SEE) p. 21
sleep (SLEEP) p. 15

Adjectives

An **adjective** describes something

deep (DEEP) p. 15
fast (FAST) p. 17
many (MEN-ee) p. 13
other (UHTH-ur) p. 9

some (SUHM) p. 7
tall (TAWL) p. 5
thick (THIK) p. 19
this (THISS) pp. 11, 21

23

What Do You See on the Prairie?

Match the Words to the Pictures

badger
bison
grass
grasshopper